From the Dust

JESSY EASTON

Lindsey -
Thank you so much for
supporting me and giving
your time to read these stories
about my life. I can't wait to
share the full book with you
one day. ♡

xo -
Jessy Easton

A collection of stories from the desert
with songs by Perry Rhodes

"Why don't you write about it?" Perry said.
"About what?" I asked.
"This. Your life. Everything."
"Why would anyone want to read about that?"
"Because a piece of it is in all of us."

This is for the children of the fallen and the brokenhearted, the brothers and sisters of the outcasts, the mothers of the lost, and the fathers of the wayward. This is for anyone who has loved someone despite the deep flaws and cracks in their being. It's for those who didn't know their place in the world, but fought like hell to find it. It's for the ones who have lived off hope because without it they had nothing. And something is always better than nothing, even a little something. This is that little something.

Contents

Introduction   ix

The Scent of Books   1

California Strays   25

I Should've Known Better   43

Flames and the Tin Foil   59

Acknowledgements   77

"All that struggles in the darkness ain't always wrong."

— Perry Rhodes

Introduction

Sometimes you have to drudge through the mud for the people you love. You have to wade through a whole mess of dark places to find what you're searching for, but it's there if you search hard enough. And I searched like hell.

I went back to the dust of where I came from—to the godforsaken town on the edge of nowhere—to explore all the messy and dark interiors of love and life. This work of creative nonfiction, which precedes my upcoming memoir, is a crack in the door, an invitation, a tiny offering, a glimpse into the greater, more expanded truths that I will later unfold in my anticipated full-length book.

Here, take my hand. I'll lead you into the darkness and show you that even at the bottom of the black nothing, at the edge of everything, there's something special here. Something true and raw that gnaws at your bones. Something human. Something good.

If you enjoy these stories, subscribe to my mailing list at jessyeaston. com/lovenotes to be alerted about the release date of my memoir. I can't wait to share it with you.

The Scent of Books

First Polaroid. Loma Linda Hospital, 1986

The Scent of Books

———————

"As happens sometimes, a moment settled and hovered
and remained for much more than a moment. And sound
stopped and movement stopped for much,
much more than a moment."

— John Steinbeck, *Of Mice and Men*

Feeling the edge of the pages under my thumbs, I search for the middle, or something that feels like the middle. Spreading the pages, I listen to the spine crack. I bring the book up to my face. Feeling the paper on my cheeks, I nestle my nose into the crease.

Inhale.

My chest fills with air and tiny specks of paper dust. I close my eyes. The inhale tapers off and my chest shudders like it's struggling to expand.

Exhale.

Is this the middle? I'm thirty, so this could quite possibly be somewhere near the middle. Maybe closer to the beginning, but how? So much has happened. And yet, not much has changed. With her, I mean. Not much has changed with her.

Her being the ever-long hurricane that is my mother. The storm that rips up the roots of my being, leaving me to stand on uneven ground, full of trenches and ruts. The scent of broken earth, of sage brush and creosote, of salt and brine from the long since dried up salt lake in the distance.

The scent of desperation.

Desperate for her to change. For her to be the mother I was robbed of as a child. She's a bright balloon that floats just out of reach. My outstretched fingers pulsing like tiny hearts, left empty and aching.

Would it always be like this? With her, I mean. With Mom. Left in the wake of her arrival and departure, staring down at my empty hands. Is this how it would always feel? Left searching for her love and for the love I gave her, the love she let spill out onto the desert floor. Left scooping up the remains, rushing to soak up every drop before it soaks into the cracked earth.

I bring the book down to my lap and go back to the beginning. The spine cracks again. I explore the first few pages for a note left by someone before me. It's there. On the inside cover in the left-hand corner, written at a diagonal in blue ink.

"Know that you are loved in Seattle Too."

Capital T.

The best thing about used books, finding sentiments like this. Frozen in time. A portal into someone else's life, what they think and how they write. Should I be here? It's too late. I've crossed the threshold. I stay awhile, thinking of the one who loves from Seattle. And the one who is loved by someone in Seattle. A story before I embark on the story itself.

I think of the stories Mom lived before I came into her world.

The story of a little girl with eyes that turned black when she got mad, who never cried because no one would hear her even if she had, who woke up to a sleeping house of strangers. Only they weren't strangers, they were her parents. But she didn't believe them, so she took off at three a.m. on a horse named Autumn against the pelting desert rain.

The story of the man with no face. She floated out from under her covers to the floor and her bedroom door opened to the grim reaper. The next morning, she fell asleep tying her shoes and she didn't wake up for three days. A bad trip? Or something more?

The story of the raid. Handcuffed by the D.E.A. alongside one of the biggest meth manufacturers in all of San Bernardino County. His name was David and he was in love with her, but so was every man she'd ever met. But none of them could tame her. Not even Dad, whose name is tattooed above her left breast. "Joseph" in faded green ink. She destroyed his life, but Dad loved her the most, and that's how I made my way into her story when she was twenty-three.

Bringing the book back up to my face, I inhale again into the crease. The scent is dry, but sweet like peaches that have been left out on the old picnic table in the sun. The picnic table from when I was a kid. From when I had grass stains on my jeans, tangles in my hair, and hands sticky with the juice of peaches.

The scent of summer.

The summer when Mom was away in state prison for the third time (or was it the second?) and Dad dropped us kids—my brother and me— off at our grandparents' house in the middle of nowhere Michigan. He drove off, past the corn fields of middle America, back through the red rocks of the southwest, to the place he called home in the Mojave Desert of California. I didn't see him for three months. I didn't see Mom for longer.

Mom lifted the edges of the window screen with her nicotine-stained fingers. The man inside saw her frail silhouette against the sunlight that poured in through the window. He dialed 911 and waited with a loaded shotgun. The police lights splashed into the desert sky and washed out the sun. The screech of tires on the hot asphalt. The clicking as the notches on the handcuffs closed around her tiny bones.

Attempted residential burglary. Sentenced to six years state prison.

The burning rubber, the sweat running from her hairline down her spine, the cold steel rubbing her wrists raw, and the latex-covered hands that searched her.

The scent of lost freedom.

My weeping face dissolved from her mind as she approached the prison—one hundred and twenty acres surrounded by razor wire and guards with guns.

The landscape of my childhood was not free, full of color and wishing flowers—but the absence of it. The slamming of heavy doors and the beeping of metal detectors. The jingling of keys from the hip of every guard and the thumping of their heavy boots in the long hallways. The fluorescent lights and the invisible ink stamped on the inside of my wrist. Cloudy panes of bulletproof glass and the cries of separated families.

The scent of waiting.

When Mom came out from behind the guarded doors, light cracked the once-sullen air like a thunderstorm. Part of me wanted to seek shelter from the havoc she could cause, but the other part was so mesmerized by her beauty and power that I couldn't help but fall into the embrace of her chaos.

I spread my stick-figure drawings of our broken family across the visiting table that wobbled and rocked. Mom pulled the last cigarette from her pack of Marlboros and shoved the empty carton under the table's stammering leg. She traced the lines on the page with the tips of her slender fingers.

"How come your dad's head is cut off?" Mom asked.

"Because he's so tall. I couldn't fit him on the paper."

Dad let out a loud, vibrant laugh. It exploded from his chest as if it surprised him, like he didn't know it was coming or that it was ever inside of him. It surprised me, too. I hadn't heard him laugh since Mom went away.

My brother asked why he was the only one I'd colored in with crayons.

"Because you always wear clothes that don't match," I said.

Mom said she liked how her hands were bigger than her body. I told her that's because I had to fit all of the rings on her fingers.

Before she was taken away, her fingers were staircased with stolen rings, one on top of the other like the books by my bedside. I liked to feel the jagged peaks of the diamonds against my skin when she'd hold my scared little hand in the dark.

I wrapped myself up in the storm of her, but the leaving always came. Sheets of tears fell heavy like storm rains and I held onto Mom until all the blood drained from my fingers. Gripping for my life, the life I was missing by not being with her.

Dad pried up each little finger glued to her arm, revealing the little white fingerprints I'd left on her skin. He held me in his long arms and I pressed my crying face against his wet cheek, feeling the heat of his tears as they blended into mine.

The mourning on my lips, the apologies she shouted into the weighted air, the grief-spurred thumping radiating from Dad's chest into my writhing bones.

The scent of leaving.

Sliding the pages across my cheeks, I pull the book away from my face. I open it again and flip to the page opposite the title page and search for the copyright date.

Copyright, 1937, by John Steinbeck.

I have a thing about dates. I like to know how long it's been since things began. Going back in time, to the beginning, the beginning of something. The beginning of what? Maybe to the beginning when my r's still sounded like w's. When radio sounded like wadio and raid came out like waid. When the cops broke the door off its hinges and raided our little house on Michelle Lane in the dust of California. Mom was taken away in handcuffs. So was Dad.

They let Dad go a few days later because the fingerprints they found all over the homes in San Bernardino County belonged to Mom. Three hundred houses and counting.

Back to the beginning. The start of measuring the years in prison sentences and release dates. Back to marking days on the calendar with sloppy red X's. Days until I could see her again.

First sentence, 1989.

Right back in, 1992.

Back again, 1993.

In and out and back again. Thousands of permanent red X's. Lost days.

Or maybe earlier, going back to the beginning of love. The love I was born out of. The love I felt from the very beginning, from Mom and Dad, for their love of drugs and for their love of us kids.

Born nine weeks early at 2:36 a.m. on the fifth of June to two people who weren't prepared for my arrival. I was gray like the June Gloom that always hit our California skies.

June. I wish they would've named me June. The halfway point in a year, the middle of the seasons. June. One hand stretched toward the light, the other reaching back for the darkness.

My lungs weren't fully developed, and I lived in a plastic bubble in order to breathe. I couldn't leave the hospital until I weighed five pounds. Three months of needles, feeding tubes, and beeping machines. The scent of alcohol, metal, and dead air. Iodoform and sick babies.

The scent of fighting like hell for your place in the world.

It was September before I got to join the outside world. The world of my parents.

Her world. The world of polluted skies and drug deals on just about every corner. The world of burglaries and carjackings. The world of methamphetamines.

Smoking. Snorting. Slamming.

Her world. Her drug of choice.

When I was young—not feeding-tube young, but young enough that I still carried around a tattered piece of Mom's red lingerie as a security blanket and a bottle filled with Coca-Cola—I'd put my little finger in the bend of her arm where the skin looked like a swirl of watercolors, blues and purples like a fading bruise. A permanent reminder of the demons she's been fighting for me all along.

In and out and back again.

I got a letter from Mom. The envelope was red. It said "W-34413" in the upper left-hand corner. Her inmate number. "W" for women and "34413" for the 34,413th inmate to be received at the prison.

First line: Hi, my darling.

Last line: I'll see you soon.

Soon being in six weeks when we'd get approval from the prison warden to visit her.

On the flap of the envelope, over the seal laced with her saliva, she wrote "I miss you" in her perfect handwriting.

I miss you Too, Mom.

Capital T.

The scent of ink, of dried glue, and spit.

The scent of yearning.

I flip through the worn pages of Steinbeck's *Of Mice and Men*. Flashes of black underlines skim by like highways to other worlds and the faded gold of highlighted sentiments flicker like stars. I follow the lines and blocks of gold into worlds that aren't my own until I come across a sentence that brings me home.

"I got you to look after me, and you got me to look after you, and that's why."

Growing up, I'd always wanted to feel looked after, but there often wasn't anyone to do the looking after. With Mom serving felony charges, Dad had to take care of us kids and the bills that piled up on the dusty kitchen table. He disappeared into the meth lab he built in the garage of our sun-bleached house. Unnoticed on the corner of a godforsaken town off the old Route 66 in California.

Dad would get so strung out he'd be up for weeks, but I didn't know the difference. I didn't notice the dark circles under his fading gray eyes, the sharp ridge of his shoulders poking through his baggy t-shirt like a coat hanger, or the extra holes he'd made in his belt with a screwdriver to hold his pants up.

I only noticed his absence—and hers. And the scent of wet paint, bleach, and cat urine.

The scent of methamphetamines.

Loss of appetite. Loss of sleep. Loss of her.

The scent of loss.

To escape the jaw-clenching silence and meth fumes seeping through the walls, we—my brother and me—wandered outside into the desert wasteland, disquiet among the tumbleweeds.

Waiting. For what? For her. For Dad to come back to us, to laugh again. For the wind to stop smacking our faces. For dinner.

Eternal waiting.

I run my finger again across that sentiment held in the gold bar of ink. I bring the page to my nose. The scent of drying paint thinner, diesel fuel, the invisible ink that stained the inside of my wrist.

Visitor. Alien. Transient.

The scent of having no home.

I read it again, running the soft flesh of my finger over the words.

"I got you to look after me, and you got me to look after you, and that's why."

I found someone who was good at doing the looking after. But when I found him, he, too, needed to be looked after.

So, we looked after each other. *That's why.*

Homeless and struggling, Perry was staying at an artist commune next to the Los Angeles River in downtown. Paint on his shoes, whiskey on his breath, and sleeplessness under his eyes.

The scent of creation.

The skin that spread across the bones of his shoulders was splattered with blemishes, swatches of varying shades of red—a reaction to the stained and soiled couch he slept on, a map sprawled across his shoulders of the life he's lived.

I traced up the ridges of his spine, through the field of imperfections dotted across his frame like the unwanted blooms of dandelions. My hands were lost in the dark sea of his wild curls. Curls that looked like Mom's.

His sad black eyes. The suffocating layers of loneliness. His wandering nature. The lines he blurred. The darkness that haunted him. It felt comforting and familiar. It felt like Mom. It felt like home.

Perry filled the gaping hole she'd left in my being. We didn't have to define who or what we were. We just were. We soaked up the thoughts of one another like the cholla cactus after a rain. Wordless, but understood.

He moved in with me, into my crumbling apartment by the marina on the west side of the city. The air was always wet and filled with the creaking of boats. The constellation that once spread across Perry's shoulders had disappeared like the stars in our light-polluted sky.

Legs intertwined, we listened to the sea birds in the mist and read the words of our favorite poets well into the dark, until our eyes squinted and burned, until morning came into the room and kissed our eyelids. The scent of the coast and the sunset-colored bougainvillea made its way into our dreams.

The scent of something true. The scent of home.

I found a home in Perry. In the soft space between his temple and his cheekbone. In the way his facial hair feels like the brittle grass of winter against my skin. In the way he reaches for me. In the way he sings me his sad songs. In the way he rests his head in my lap while I read to him. In the way he gives me the quiet space I need to write. In the way he sees me. In the way he makes me feel free.

Closing the book, I study its spine. It's creased and the dried glue peels and sheds like the bark of a melaleuca tree.

In one vivid rush of memory, I see its faded spine in the little bookshop off Valencia Street in San Francisco. It laid on the bottom shelf. I already had five copies, but I couldn't help myself. Each one is different with its own story attached to it from the lives it has touched before mine.

Perry reached his hand out to me, palm up—like Dad always used to do—to where I sat on the floor with the books on the bottom shelf. I slid my hand into his. I felt the calluses that built up on his fingertips from playing the steel resonator guitar I bought him for Christmas one year. He pulled me to my feet and kissed my cheek.

"Whatcha got there?" he asked, glancing at the book in my hand.

"A gift," I said, burying myself in his thrift store coat that was worlds too big for his shoulders, but somehow still looked like it was made for him.

It was raining. We walked the streets of the Mission District with books in our bags and dreams in our heads. Big dreams of lives better than what we started with, better than the beginnings that were handed to us. Dreams of space, a physical space and a mental one, a space in our hearts to create. To create a life that was ours. To create a home.

We watched the threads of lightning explode through the glow of the streetlights. The air smelled wet, of asphalt and gasoline, of mint and honey from the blue gum eucalyptus, and of tortillas from the damp steam wafting out of the taquerias.

The water seeped through the soles of my scuffed leather shoes and collected at the ends of Perry's curls. His eyelashes were thick and wet, and I licked the raindrops from his face.

This was long after our beginning, well after our escape, and after our starting over.

We both fled from where we began, from the wake of dust. To the city. To tall buildings and opportunities. To record labels and album deals. To freedom. Or what we thought freedom was.

We signed on the dotted line.

His name scribbled with big capital letters, followed by a line, a squiggle. Illegible, but binding to the record label to create an album, to tour, to do what they said.

Twelve tracks. Two singles. Stadiums. MTV.

London. Munich. Paris. Bangkok. Manilla. Through state lines, across America.

The scent of microphones and truck-stop bathrooms, sweat laden with alcohol, jet fuel and late-night fast-food runs.

The scent of making it.

My name signed in cursive, neat like Mom's. I signed my legal name. Jessica. It felt like I was signing as someone else, as no one had called me that since I was a kid on welfare in line for free lunch.

"Easton, Jessica," the lunch lady would shout. She might as well have stamped POOR on my forehead.

I signed Jessica on the dotted line, but told them to call me Jess or Jessy, please, if you don't mind. I'd pick up the phone at my desk on the second floor of the Atlantic Records building on Olive Avenue.

"Publicity, this is Jessy."

Rolling Stone. The Los Angeles Times. Entertainment Weekly. Vogue.

They wanted interviews. Show tickets. Their names on the guest lists.

The scent of magazine pages and bottle service, of nicotine and greenrooms, of expensive leather and the Sunset Strip.

The scent of empty promises.

Turns out, we weren't free.

We turned our backs on the music industry, not music itself, but the business of it.

The scent of empty apartments and cardboard boxes, of plane tickets, and a blank page.

The scent of starting over.

The starting over had its own beginning. The beginning of us, Perry and me. The us that was free. The us that spread ourselves across the page, sliding off the dotted line, and into our dreams. The us that left Los Angeles, the city of dreams, the city of oranges.

One-way flight to Hawaii. The scent of sulfur from the volcanic fog and the soft flesh of young coconuts. Salt and sea and the pulp of coffee cherries.

The scent of escape.

We slept under the stars in the mango orchards while the mosquitos feasted on our California blood. "I thought it'd be sweeter," they'd said.

We traded in the warmth and the black sand for wet cobblestone streets and languages that weren't ours.

Lying in Paris, in the third story of an apartment owned by a woman named Claudia, I listened to the energy flowing beneath me on Rue Montorgueil.

The scent of coffee before my eyes opened, of sex in the copper light, and the night's one-too-many cognacs.

The scent of morning.

I touch my nose to the crease of the book's spine. Inhaling the pages like they give me life. They do. Flipping through, I find a letter from Mom, folded eight times.

First line: I just want to tell you how very much I love you and how much I'm going to miss you.

Last line: Have fun, don't worry, and I'll be waiting for you with the same love I've always had for you.

"I'll be waiting for you," she wrote.

I've spent my life waiting for her. Forever slipping through my fingers like water.

Eternal waiting. Forever fleeting.

I fan through the pages of the book, holding it in the air. The pages flutter like the weary wings of tiny birds. Something falls. A glimmer. Silent like snow fall. I reach for it. Delicate in my fingers. Heavy in my heart, but weightless in my hands. Flat and clear like an unbroken sea.

A tiny bag of destruction. Flimsy plastic like a sandwich bag. I found them in Mom's jewelry box, in her makeup bag, in the inside zipper pocket of her purse, in the cracks of the plum-colored couch that sits in her garage. Maybe they were hidden in her curls. If only I would've checked.

This one, I had once used as a bookmark during the last time I visited her in the soul-crushing town she still calls home. I found it on the windowsill of her bathroom under an empty bottle of cheap perfume. It was empty and clean.

Unlike the one I found in her jewelry box on Christmas morning.

Unlike the one I found in Dad's jacket pocket the night before it snowed. The one she lied about and said was his. Unlike the one I found in her makeup bag when she was in the hospital with a broken foot from kicking down the door of a house she was attempting to rob. Unlike the one I found on the floor in the garage next to the tin foil stains in the carpet.

The burning of lighter fluid, the flickering of the flame, the meth fog that collects along the edges of the blanket-covered windows.

The scent of survival.

The Scent of books

San Francisco
and chemistry
threads of lightning
amphetamines
I'd keep it all together
but that aint workin anymore

were we coffee
or morphine
the scent of books
or old melodies
I'd hide out in those pages
but that aint workin anymore

don't ever change
watching your beauty running off
in those street lights
gettin covered in rain

were we neon writhing
or ecstasy
the blood still burning
or just apologies
I'd keep it all together
but that aint workin anymore

don't ever change
watching your beauty running off
in those street lights
gettin covered in rain

don't ever change
we were just books
left out in the night sky
gettin covered in rain

some things never change

—Perry Rhodes 2019

Lyrics. Perry Rhodes, 2019

Devonshire Road, San Bernardino, 1992

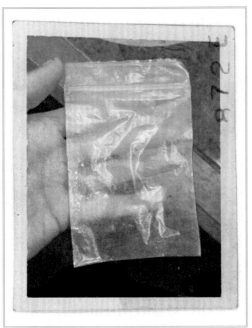

Smoke Tree Road, Victorville, 2012

Beginnings. San Bernardino, 1984

Devonshire Road, San Bernardino, 1992

The first time. San Bernardino, 1989

Letter to prison. Chowchilla, 1994

Film by Katch Silva, Joshua Tree, 2017

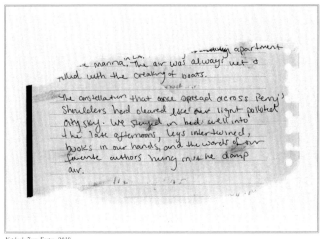

... manna in LA. The air was always wet &
filled with the creaking of boats.

The constellation that once spread across Perry's
shoulders had cleared like our light polluted
city sky. We stayed in bed well into
the late afternoons, legs intertwined,
books in our hands, and the words of our
favorite authors hung in the damp
air.

Notebook. Jessy Easton, 2019

California Strays

El Rio Road, Victorville, 1994

California Strays

———

"Memories warm you up from the inside. But they also tear you apart."

— Haruki Murakami, *Kafka on the Shore*

His words rushed in, swallowing up my hope in huge gulps.

"Fuck, Tammy. What am I supposed to tell the kids?"

It was dark when the phone rang, and Dad had been banging around in the kitchen trying to find something to feed us. The whole room went silent, and I felt the mood shift as he held the phone to his ear.

It was happening, again.

This was Mom's third time in prison. I was seven, my brother Brandon, six. We lived in a beige house with stucco on the outside and tumbleweeds in the front yard on the corner of Arroyo Drive in Victorville where the desert feeds off the hopeless.

With Mom gone, the Arroyo house seemed so much darker and quieter. The light could never find its way through the blankets that hung from nails over every window. Dad stopped picking up, so the sink overflowed with dishes, and old newspapers and late notices covered every chair and counter. Sometimes Brandon and I would write bad words in the thick layer of dust coating the dining table just to make each other laugh.

The laughing, it was fleeting. Like everything good has always been. I slumped and sulked all over the house and dragged myself through the days that stretched on for centuries. My dark eyes haunted by sleeplessness, I spent long hours sitting in our driveway waiting for Mom to come home. Time went on forever in every direction and it was so damn quiet. I'd listen to the growl of my stomach as the wind beat against the sad creosote bushes and whipped my tangled blonde hair around like a dust tornado.

As I watched the light bend over the asphalt, it played tricks on my mind, creating shimmering mirages that looked like just Mom's silver car. She always had a giant crystal hanging from her rearview mirror that shot specks of brilliant light around like an explosion of confetti.

I thought maybe if I hoped hard enough, or waited long enough, she would show up. And when I'd hear the sound of a motor in the distance, I'd lift my head and squint into the white sun to see if it was her. Maybe if I kept waiting, kept looking, I'd spot her wild black curls through the window or the crystal's glittering light. I never did. But I didn't have anything if I didn't have hope—I held on to it so tight I just about strangled it.

Dad told me to stop sitting around feeling sorry for myself, so I attempted to push Mom out of my mind, and I mourned her absence for the thousandth time. Dad was right, though. Anything was better than dwelling on the waiting.

Brandon abated my loneliness by dragging me out into the desert wasteland next to our house for his adventures of fighting off imaginary bad guys and searching for buried treasure. We created games out of thin air, leaping across the fallen Joshua trees because we imagined the desert floor as lava. Jumping from tree to tree, it was just my brother and me among the dust and the rattlesnakes, living in a world we dreamed up.

We walked for miles without seeing another soul. Coming across some old junk some desert-dwellers left behind—a ripped up chair with the insides pouring out, empty beer cans, and a naked and bald mannequin—we brought the mannequin home to show Dad. He said he'd use it for target practice. He had a bunch of guns in a steel locker in the corner of his bedroom. Loading up a shotgun and a couple of handguns, we drove deep into the desert, crushing the tumbleweeds and Mojave asters under our tires along the way. Dad shot holes in the mannequin until there was nothing left of her. We stuffed our fingers in our ears, jumping and cheering with every shot he fired.

It was days like those that my mind gave up thinking about Mom. But then night would come, and Dad would vanish into the garage for what felt like an eternity. I'd lay in his lonely waterbed on Mom's side and pretend the rocking of the water was the rise and fall of her body beside me as she breathed.

I'd melt into the curves of her bones and by morning it would be as if my body had fused with hers, like the tide swallowing up a lonely sand-castle. The rest of the world shut out from our existence. She was my safe place. Until she went away, and I was left alone with the shadow without a face and the things that lurked beyond the green.

Dad had a secret camera that watched over the front door and the feed ran into a monitor in his room. It buzzed and hummed on a dusty shelf at the end of his bed. With heavy eyelids I begged for sleep, but when I shut my eyes, I could still see the bright green glow of the night cam feed. What existed within the black and green monitor crawled along in my mind until I couldn't help but fall into a glaze in front of the screen.

The shades of green created shadows on the bedroom walls. The coats that hung on the back of the door turned into the grim reaper. The lamp shade created a shadow on the ceiling that was ready to devour me. I trembled, afraid of closing my eyes or keeping them open. A fog of panic felt as if it were going to smother me.

I wasn't supposed to disrupt Dad when he was *working* unless I had a good reason. I knew that my irrational fear of nothing would just make me look like a whiner—and Dad hated whiners—but I panicked.

I sat up and slid to the edge of the bed, my bare feet dangling as the waterbed sloshed beneath me. I tiptoed from his room down the dark hallway to the door of the garage. I stood there for a moment trying to find the strength to go back to bed, but I couldn't grasp it. Time stood still and I shivered in the deafening silence.

With bed head, clenched fists, and dark circles under my eyes, my heart pounded heavy in my chest. I felt like I was standing on the edge of time. I brought my hand up to knock, skin and bone against pine.

"Daddy…" I said in a worn whisper. Part of me didn't want him to hear me, but the other part of me knew that I couldn't leave until he did. "Daddy," I said again. I stood there, empty, waiting for the door to swing open. "I can't sleep," I said into the crack of the doorjamb.

The door flew open and the misty gold light from the garage flooded my face. Dad towered over me and let out a weighted sigh. Putting his hand on my head, he directed me back to the green glow. A foggy odor seeped in from the garage, down the ill-lit hallway, and into the bedroom where it collected along the edges of the blanket nailed over the window above Dad's waterbed. I shuffled through the mess along the bedroom floor—a broken Sega controller that I'd destroyed in one of my rage-filled tantrums, an empty box of Pop-Tarts, Dad's black-and-red flannel, old copies of *Guns & Ammo* magazine, and a tube of Gillette deodorant— and climbed back onto the bed.

"You know you have nothing to be scared of," he said.

His eyes looked vacant and I could see the sharp hitch of his shoulders. I knew I had frustrated him with my weakness. I looked down at the dirt under my fingernails to avoid his eyes. Dad held out his hand and I placed mine in the middle of his giant cracked palm. The tips of his fingers were speckled with a faded rusty orange color from the iodine he used to make meth. He closed his hand around mine and I thought about how the stains looked just like the carrot juice Grandma Linda would make for us in Michigan sometimes.

"You know I'd never let anything bad happen to you." He cupped my sweating hands in his.

My fearful eyes rushed with comfort. "Can you stay here? Just until I fall asleep."

Dad nodded and his unbrushed hair fell in his face. The circles under his eyes were complete darkness. They looked as if he'd spent his whole life fighting sleep.

He sat at the end of the bed playing a video game and the shadows returned to being only shadows. Releasing my clenched fists, I stretched my arms out and felt something cold and foreign in the bed beside me, but I couldn't make out what it was. I lifted up the pillow. It was Dad's gun. I turned away from it onto Mom's side and watched Dad's black silhouette in the green haze. I fell asleep to the clicking of the Sega controller.

I don't know how long it had been, but Dad was gone when I woke up and I was left with the buzzing of the green glow. The video game he'd been playing when I fell asleep was paused on the screen. *Streets of Rage.* I'd been sleeping on my arm and it felt like little stars were twinkling inside my palm.

The nights were always the same.

I'd spend the the dark hours being pushed around by my fear, imprisoned by the cloak of blackness until I couldn't take it anymore.

Then one night I turned the handle to the door of the garage.

I tried to knock, but Dad didn't hear the tapping. Opening the door, I squinted into the fluorescent fog and tiptoed through the little paths carved out of rows of junk. A room of hallways.

But no Dad.

Plastic sheeting splattered with black paint hung down from the ceiling in the corner like a crime scene of dried blood. A generator laid out in parts that were polished chrome, so shiny I could see my reflection. Tools hung on the wall by rusty nails above Dad's workbench and a hose hung from the ceiling down into a blue cooler. Jugs of distilled water lined the floor and tins of acetone and camp fuel filled the shelves along the side wall.

His shotgun with the long barrel sat propped up against the workbench next to a giant book that laid open with a bullet hole though the middle of the pages. I tried to lift it to look through the hole, but it was too heavy. It slipped out of my hands and onto the top of my foot. I gasped and folded over my knees, clutching my foot. It had its own heartbeat. That's when I noticed the shattered glass on the floor by the workbench and the beakers that laid on their side next to the battery-operated fan that still hummed in the corner. Besides the spinning of the fan, the room was still.

Or I thought it was.

Until I saw the ceiling dripping and the clear liquid streaming down the walls like tears. It smelled like cat urine cleaned with bleach, spray paint, and the nail salon I used to go to with Mom. My nose stung and my eyes burned and blurred. Tears welled up against the stench and I heard the slamming of a car door. I didn't know if it was Dad, but he'd throw himself into a yelling fit full of curses if he found me in the garage.

I made my way out as Dad was walking down the hallway from the living room. Standing in the threshold of his room, the green glow spilled out from behind me onto his floating shadow in the hallway. I watched his heavy steel-toed boots drag his wilting frame into the garage.

Back to the rocking of the water.

The green glow buzzed.

I felt the sea beneath me and in one wash of memory I could taste the salt on my lips and see where the water foamed at our toes.

Dad had driven us to the sea to distract us from the fact that a whole person was missing from our lives. Dust wafted up from the seat when I sat down and it smelled like sun and motor oil. It smelled like Dad. A stream of light poured through the windshield streaked with dust and bird shit. I looked up at Dad. His eyes, the color of rainclouds, were squinting and I watched the fluttery shadows on his sharp cheekbones dance with each blink from his long eyelashes. He had one hand on the steering wheel and the other laid palm up in my lap. I had ahold of his giant calloused fingers that were stained with tire grease.

I slid across the cracked leather seats when Dad took the corner and grabbed ahold of his fingers with both hands. Old Snapple bottles clanked under my feet in the footwell. Brandon was sitting in the back seat because I'd called shotgun.

He slid his head between us. "Dad! She never lets me sit in the front seat."

"Tough shit. Put your seatbelt back on and quit your whining," Dad said.

We drove through the burned and burning hills of California and tried to pass the time playing I Spy, only it was hopeless because we were in the middle of a dust-filled sky and all the colors were varying shades of beige. I could feel the hum of the engine through my seat when the world went gray and I fell into the sleeping realm. My head bounced off the window with every bump of the road. Then the engine stilled, and I woke to the sound of sea birds. Brandon was asleep in the footwell of the backseat and the ocean was outside our window.

I tossed Skittles at him until he stirred. He popped his head up and saw the sand-strewn coast.

"We're here," I said.

Dad swung the door open and it creaked at the hinges. He said he'd race us to the shoreline on the count of three. One. Two. Dad took off running, his big laugh cracking the sky. We pounded the sand, feeling it slide between our toes, and swallowed the salt of the air in hurried breaths.

Dad turned around and stood at the edge of everything with his arms wide like wings and we hurled ourselves against him. Scooping us up, he went running into the waves where sand and dreams were serenades. Touching the soles of our feet to the looking glass, the salt crept up the hems of our jeans. Then he let go.

My toes touched down onto the ocean floor with each gentle swell. I watched Brandon splashing around, doing his best dog paddle. Dad had disappeared under the wall of green and I felt around in the black weeds of the sea for his soaking bones. Then I looked past the water and Dad was kneeling at the rim of the shore, threading water through his long hair.

I let the tide carry me to him kneeling in the sand. He looked lighter, like a great weight had been lifted from his shoulders. I brought my palms up to his face and flattened them against his wet cheeks. He covered my hands with his and I wanted to cry because for a breath, we'd fallen into an accidental moment of joy.

Dad cupped the cool Pacific in his hands and flung the sea onto my face. It smelled like the pulp of the ocean and the salt stained my cheeks. Dad laughed and it was carried off into the blue where the wind never sleeps. I reached after it, but it frayed in my tiny fingers.

Brandon was still a bobbing head among the waves, his thick wet hair the color of cinnamon sticking out every which way like he was a ball of static. The day was already starting to blue when Dad called him out to meet us on the brim where the lonely shells scattered up and down the coast. I watched Brandon wallow out from the neck-deep green. He sniffled and coughed the sea into his shriveled hands.

Dad handed me a rotting piece of wood he found half-sticking out of the wet earth.

"Here, write something to your Mom," he said.

I dripped salt and shivered in the blue evening as I held the spongy bark in my hand. I scrawled "I love you" with hearts for o's and listened to the whisper of the sand against the words. Brandon wrote "Hi Mom" and waved to the camera. Snap. Dad clicked the shutter and sent our love to the stars like the universe was listening.

Stretching his arms up like night birds against the failed light of the moon, Dad tossed the branch back into the ocean. The violent pulse of the sea made a mock of our hearts. I swear we once were starry eyed, but the afternoon turned to black, erasing the line between the sky and the sea, and I forgot where I was. A darkness bleeding into a greater darkness. I scanned the windswept coast searching for hope, but all I found was desperation.

I stumbled into whatever the universe had left to give, but the shoreline was just the edge of my sorrow. In and out and back again. The sea crawled over the love I'd written in the sand and flowed back out, devouring the words, wiping the earth clean of her. The crashing of the water intertwined with the flickering drum in my chest as I watched the long silhouettes of Dad and Brandon dissolve into the dark.

I looked away from the surface of the black toward the lights along the boardwalk that looked like the glowing glances of night creatures. I shut my eyes to them, but I could still see the glimmer of their brightness thread underneath my lashes.

The glow pried at my eyelids and everything went green.

The rocking of the waterbed cradled my sea-beaten heart and the buzzing of the monitor sent a shudder through my salt-sheened bones.

Oh, how I strayed, but never far enough.

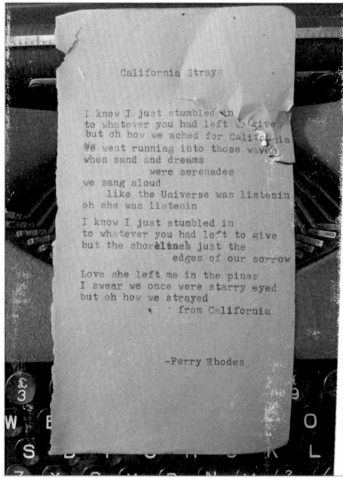

California Strays

I know I just stumbled in
to whatever you had left to give
but oh how we ached for California
We went running into those waves
when sand and dreams
          were serenades
we sang aloud
     like the Universe was listenin
oh she was listenin

I know I just stumbled in
to whatever you had left to give
but the shorelines just the
               edges of our sorrow

Love she left me in the pines
I swear we once were starry eyed
but oh how we strayed
          from California

                    -Perry Rhodes

Lyrics, Perry Rhodes, 2018

Arroyo Drive, Victorville, 1993

Photobooth. Victorville, 1993

The desert. Victorville, 1993

The beach. Laguna, 1993

· The world tilted and I was at the sea
· ~~piece the looking glass~~
· Ice cream stained sleeves, sticky fingers, and
a ring of sugar around our mouths.
· ~~I tasted teeny, not~~ I'd turn into a new way ~~of~~
~~me floured and devoured itself.~~ happy
· The lonely shells of the sea scattered up
and down the shoreline.
· black weeds of the sea, coiled and twined
· ~~tint of the waves~~
· The dividing line almost invisible, a blue
against a greater blue. → Then the night
came in again and erased the line between the
sky and sea — a blackness bleeding into an
even greater blackness.
· ~~I swear.~~

Notebook. Jessy Easton, 2019

Michelle Lane, San Bernardino, 1989

I Should've Known Better

West Valley Detention Center, Rancho Cucamonga

I Should've Known Better

"What a loss to spend that much time with someone, only
to find out that she's a stranger."

— Joel Barish in *Eternal Sunshine of the Spotless Mind*
by Charlie Kaufman

Mom was always glowing, be it from the day's sun, the fluorescent
lights of the prison visiting ward, the flickering of the lighter flame, or the
police lights shooting around her like dying stars. On this night, it was the
glow from the porch light that illuminated her.

I was visiting from college for the weekend, back in the desert for the
millionth time. The living room was dim and I was lying on the plum-colored couch watching *Eternal Sunshine of the Spotless Mind* to distract myself
from being back in the Mojave. As I started to lose myself in the surreal-
ism of the film, I heard a knock at the door. Jarred by the sound, I fought
the urge to fold into myself. There it was again. A knock against the edge
of the old screen door that sounded more like a tapping.

Tap. Tap. Tap.

My chest went tight with dread like it was filling up with water.
Nothing good ever came from the tap, tap, tap. I forced myself toward
the sound. Two figures stood beyond the screen. They blurred into the
night behind them and I squinted trying to make out their faces. The
glare of their badges on their chests lit my limbs on fire.

My hands, pale and trembling, reached for the door. It creaked when
I opened it, but I could only hear the ringing in my ears. Watching the

shadows of moths move across their stiff faces, I opened my mouth to speak, but no words came out.

"Is Tammy Easton home?" one of them asked.

I should've known.

I could see his lips moving but the words sounded foreign, from another country, another planet. I don't know how long I stood there voiceless, staring at his flapping mouth, but it felt like all of eternity.

"Miss, is Tammy Easton home?" he asked again. His lips were chapped and the slivers of dried skin peeled and flaked along the edges of his mouth.

The words were beginning to form in my mind and all the blood left my body, leaving me lifeless like a bag of bones.

"Miss, we need to speak with her. Is she home?"

Dad came out from the kitchen and saw the cops through the crack in the screen. "What's going on?" he asked.

I disappeared behind Dad, burying my face into the small of his back. He smelled like warm laundry and defeat. I felt the thunder of fear run through him when he let out a sigh. Muffled tears rushed out of me and soaked the back of his shirt and he reached his hand around to me crumbling behind him.

"Sir, is Tammy Easton home?"

Dad cleared his throat and I listened as he forced down a hard gulp. I couldn't see his face, but I knew he was clenching his jaw. I was clenching mine, too, and I couldn't swallow. My mouth felt as if it had been pumped full of sand.

Mom emerged from the hallway. I could see the blood-colored sweater covering her fleeting form and the flowing darkness of her hair, but it was as if I were peering through stained glass. She wedged herself between us—Dad and me—and the uniforms at the door.

"What's up?" she asked the cops with her bottomless calm.

"Tammy Easton, we're going to need you to come with us."

Mom opened the screen door wider. Her vacant eyes bounced from one cop to the other like a pinball. She began to ask why, but the cop with the chapped lips interrupted her with his dry, little mouth.

"You're under arrest for…" He rattled on, but again I couldn't understand a word he was saying.

"No, please! You can't take her. You can't take her. You can't take her," I said over and over. My voice sounded strange in my ears like it belonged to someone else.

"Moo Moo, it's okay. They can't keep me."

Mom stepped over the threshold of our home into the unknown. I reached for her, but it was too late. They were already tightening the handcuffs around her wrists. Fear washed over me like an icy wave and chills covered my arms. Dad placed the palms of his sweating hands on my shoulders and I felt him shuddering. Or maybe it was me. Maybe it was both of us. Dad rested his heavy head on top of mine and I went weightless like the ground was being pulled out from under me. Listening to Mom's footsteps fade away from us like hushed whispers in the dark, my teeth banged together and I couldn't control my sobbing.

"Are you guys happy now?" Dad shouted to the backs of the cops.

They didn't turn around, but Mom did.

"It's going to be okay, Moo Moo. I love you," she said, looking back over her shoulder. Her face was bathed in the copper glow of the porch light; she looked like a fading flame. "Infinity times the universe double-root-squared!" she shouted, but her voice trailed away like she was falling down a deep well.

Or maybe I was the one falling.

I ran after her, but the door of the patrol car slammed shut and she was lost behind the glowing red window pane. My empty hands ached. I watched the cops pull away and the red taillights slink off into the night. Wilting onto the asphalt, I felt the sunless heat on my palms. I could hear Dad's hurried stride move toward me and his worried voice in the wind, but everything went black.

I should've known better.

Mom was in jail—again—and at first I refused to visit her. It had been over a decade since her last sentence and I thought I was done worrying about visiting hours and placing sloppy red X's on the calendar until the next time I could see her. I thought I was done having to read-just to life without her.

But Mom missed everything.

She missed my college graduation—I didn't bother going to the ceremony because what was the point? Without Mom everything seemed meaningless. Plus, what was I celebrating anyway? The crippling debt I had accrued? Yeah, let's throw a damn party.

She missed my move to Los Angeles—Dad came down and brought me Mom's couch—the plum-colored one I had been lying on when she was arrested again. He said he didn't need it, and if Mom wanted it then she shouldn't have gotten herself thrown in jail again.

And she missed my first day working at Atlantic Records—I wanted to show her the fancy keycard I got with my picture on it and the massive stack of CDs they sent me home with, including some of my favorite Led Zeppelin albums. I would've given just about anything to rock out with her to "Black Dog" that day.

I should've known better.

Instead, I lied to my colleagues and the new friends I'd made at work about where I came from and the world I'd finally escaped, the world Mom was still part of. They asked where I grew up, and I told them out in the desert near where the Coachella music festival was held every year. Victorville wasn't even in the same desert, but they didn't have to know that.

My roommate would spend the weekends hanging out with her mom at their beach condo. I'd tag along sometimes pretending that sipping mimosas on the deck and spending thirty bucks on a salad at the sea-front steakhouse was a normal thing for me to do, too. When questions about my family would surface, I'd try to spin things in a way that sounded appealing.

"What does your father do?"

"Dad spends a lot of his time working on cars. He's always had a big passion for classic cars. He used to have a cool Firebird that he fixed up himself."

"What about your mom?"

"She likes helping people. She spends a lot of time at the jail talking with women prisoners."

"Oh, that's nice of her," they'd say.

"Yeah, she has a big heart."

At least that part was true.

Working at Atlantic felt like a dream. Red carpet events with the musicians whose pictures I had ripped out of *Rolling Stone* and taped to my wall when I was in high school, after-parties on the Sunset Strip that I used to fantasize about, my name on the guest list at the Chateau Marmont and the party in the hills that no one was supposed to know about.

I finally felt like I belonged somewhere.

Every month or so I drove up from Los Angeles to visit Dad and my brother, Brandon. But things were not looking good, and Dad was looking even worse. He'd picked up drinking with the guys from the tire shop and quickly fell into swigging tequila alone in his old recliner chair. He'd pour the clear, burning liquid into a glass and I'd watch it disappear past the heavy lump in his throat. With most of Mom's stuff gone, and all of Mom gone, the house felt as if no one lived there.

I started to come up more on weekends, and on Sundays Dad and I would watch football together. I picked up drinking to feel closer to him. At least that was part of the reason. Mostly, I was trying to obliterate the part of me that was broken, to numb the raging despair of losing Mom again.

I should've known better.

Dad would often start our day of drinking at nine in the morning. Brandon said football was boring and drinking made us stupid, but we'd ignore him. I'd laugh when Dad talked back to the refs, calling them cocksuckers and saying that they didn't know shit. He'd raise his fists to the television like he was going to challenge it to a fight.

Sometimes Dad would come down to visit me in Los Angeles and we'd watch the game from a barstool. We'd put back too many tequila shots and I wouldn't remember which team won. Dad would drive the two-hours back to Victorville drunk as hell. He said he'd just close one eye if he started seeing double.

I'd go to work hungover or still drunk from the night before, but no one would notice. Or maybe they did, but didn't care because most people drank alcohol like it was water anyway. I'd slump down to the middle of my spine and fall asleep in my orange desk chair.

One day, I woke to the sound of the phone ringing.

"Publicity, this is Jessy," I answered in an I-wasn't-sleeping tone.

It was Grandma Fields—Mom's mom. She said she was sorry to call me at work, but she'd made an appointment for me to see Mom. I let out a long sigh. Grandma said Mom kept asking for me so I needed to stop being so selfish.

"She's your mother," she said. "She loves you."

"Is this what love looks like?"

She scoffed, all phlegm and rasp, and went quiet for a moment. Then she said, "She's at West Valley. Don't be late or they won't let you in."

I should've known better.

West Valley, the worst place of all. The place where Mom drowns in an oversized jumpsuit behind bulletproof glass. I pulled into the parking lot of the jail and looked out the window at the barbed wire that looked like crooked teeth. I flinched at the thought of getting out of the car. It was Mom's car, an old Pontiac Grand Prix, blinding red and fast as hell. I wanted to crash it into a brick wall at a hundred miles an hour and shatter the windshield with my bones, but I worried about what Dad would do without me.

I wished he could've been there riding shotgun next to me. I wished he could've been there to give Mom's name to the guard behind the metal speaker. I wished I could've gotten lost in his giant hand as he led me down the long fluorescent hallways. But I wasn't a kid anymore, and wishing never did me any good anyway.

I should've known better.

I closed my eyes and laid my head back against the seat. I felt nauseous in the dry heat and the stream of sun that streaked through the window burned at the edges of my eyelids. Slamming my hands down on the steering wheel, I bruised the heel of my palm. Anger roared through my body in great bursts, but it was sympathy that pulled me out of the car.

Even worse than facing the endless buzzing, the metal detectors, the guarded doors, and the eternal waiting was the thought of Mom sitting by the phone only to find out that I didn't show. I couldn't let myself abandon her like that.

I was like a well-trained animal forever waiting for the sound of the buzzer. I waited at the metal picnic table, feeling sorry for myself while a swarm of flies bit at my ankles. Folding my arms across the table, I laid my head into the crook of my elbow. The skin of my forehead felt like it had fused with the dampness of my arm and it made a sticky smacking sound when I lifted my head to the sound of the buzzer.

I stumbled through the metal detector and gave the cop my wrist to stamp with the invisible ink. I went in, down the hallway to the metal speaker, and into the tiny room lined with sad metal cubicles and heavy phones and waited for her. The air smelled like Styrofoam and the steam of microwavable soup and I tried to take long, deep breaths to keep myself from falling apart.

Buzz.

The guards opened the door and there she was, pretty as ever. But

I could only think one thing: *I should've known better.* She looked shiny and new and well-rested like she'd been on vacation. Mom smiled and brought the phone up to her ear. I stared at the soft curls that fell across her shoulders like a black cloud. *I should've known better.* Mom looked at me and I saw guilt in her misty dark eyes and I realized my own were raw and burning. *I should've known better.* She tapped on the glass, waiting for me to pick up the receiver on the other side.

Tap. Tap. Tap.

The sound sent a current through my marrow. I cringed and picked up the phone, waiting for all the lies to spill out. I wanted to scream at her and slam the receiver against the glass, but all I could force out was, "How did we end up back here?"

Lyrics. Perry Rhodes, 2019

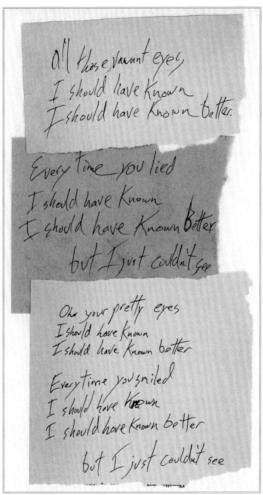

all those vacant eyes,
I should have known
I should have known better.

Every time you lied
I should have known
I should have known better
but I just couldn't see

Oh your pretty eyes
I should have known
I should have known better

Every time you smiled
I should have known
I should have known better
but I just couldn't see

Lyrics, Perry Rhodes, 2019

Better days. The desert

Sticking together. Then and now

Grief, stage four

West Valley Detention Center, Rancho Cucamonga

Flames and the Tin Foil

Devonshire Road, San Bernardino, 1984

Flames and the Tin Foil

"This thing of darkness I acknowledge mine."

— William Shakespeare, *The Tempest*

"If you knew all the bad things I've done you probably wouldn't even talk to me anymore," Mom says to me.

She's sitting on the velvet couch in the garage. The color of plums. The one she bought when she was clean. Or when I thought she was. It's now dotted with cigarette burns like a map of the decline of her. Her curls, dark as ink, drape around her face like an overgrown garden and she smells like nicotine and coffee that's been left to go cold. I watch as she pulls a lighter from her bra and lights a Marlboro Red.

I'm about to speak when a glassy veil falls over her wild, dark eyes. A memory. It sprawls across her consciousness. A story. I listen as the drags of amber light her face.

Mom was holed up in a motel room she'd paid for with a stolen credit card. Tony was with her, one of the many guys she cheated on Dad with. The dead of summer spread through the room and the paint on the walls cracked like the scales of a reptile.

Outside the window, the shadows stretched to nothing as the sun fell behind the dying strip mall across the street. Mom yanked the curtain closed and particles of dust exploded into the air. She sat at the edge of the bed hunched over a laundry basket full of stolen jewelry she'd nicked from some oversized house off Valencia Avenue. The number of houses she'd robbed was well into the three-digits.

Tony was in the bathroom and the room was a painful quiet. Mom searched through the knotted mass of gold for rings she could stack on her fingers. She slid on a yellow gold band with a blaring cluster of diamonds, twisting it back and forth in the musty dark, she studied it for sparkle and clarity.

Mom hopped off the bed and the mattress squeaked. She brought the ring underneath the shade of the lamp on the nightstand. She moved it back and forth in the yellow light and fell into a trance as she watched it shimmer.

Then the phone rang, cutting through the motel's dusty silence. Mom startled and hit the top of her hand against the lightbulb. It made a clinking sound and felt hot against her skin.

"Fuck," she said, picking up the handset and slamming it down. It made a muffled moan at the force, but the ringing ceased. Mom turned to walk away from the phone, but the ringing started up again and stopped her mid-stride. She turned around and lunged forward, reaching for it in one elongated sweep.

"What?" she huffed into the receiver.

"Ms. Barrett?"

Mom thought for a moment. *Barrett? Oh, fuck.*

"Yes, this is she," she answered with a tone of confidence.

"Hi, this is the front desk. Would you be able to please come up and show us your I.D. We need it to run your card for the room."

"Of course, no problem."

She ignored the request and sat back onto the squeaky mattress, stretching out her tired legs in front of her. She'd also stolen a fur coat from the Valencia house, and it laid on the bed like a sleeping wolf at her feet. She ran her fingers through the fur, sliding her hand into the pocket. Pulling out a bag of meth, a hollow pen, and a rectangle of tin foil folded in half and then into squares eight times, she laid everything out on the bedspread.

She smoothed out the folds of the foil with the credit card she'd stolen and folded a crease down the middle like a gutter running along a city sidewalk. Pulling her orange translucent lighter out of the pocket of her acid-wash jeans, she brought the hair of the flame to the base of the foil.

Sliding the flame up and down, always moving, until she heard the foil crackle from the heat.

Shaking the bag between her fingers with the flick of her tiny wrist, she listened to the snapping sound of the flimsy plastic. Mom pulled it open with her teeth and upended the white powder into the gutter. The click of the lighter. The orange of the flame. The inhaling of the white fog like a cold breath on winter mornings.

One. Two. Three times. The flame passes under the tin foil. In and out and back again. Inhale. The river of white. Exhale. The water at the door. It swirled and twined through the room, crawling along the bed, across the floor, up the melting walls onto the ceiling until the room was swallowed up by the rush of the current.

Mom stood up and grabbed the coat on the bed with both hands. Sliding her wasted arms along the cool, silk lining, she felt a comforting shiver even though the edge of her hairline was dabbed with sweat. Her bird-like shoulders disappeared within the carcass, and the animal skin kissed the floor. Mom felt it dragging behind her as she made her way over to the mirror. A crack in the glass frayed her reflection, but she hardly noticed.

Then the phone rang again.

Fuck, she thought, but ignored it.

Weaving her ring-covered fingers under her hair, she pulled her dark strands out from under the heavy coat collar. She smiled and her sharp cheekbones cut through the air. Twirling in the flickering motel light, the pelts followed her every sway and her curls splayed out like fireworks.

Mom noticed a red explosion behind her reflection. The flashing of cop lights bled onto the walls from the edges of the curtain.

She pounded on the bathroom door.

"The cops are here. Time to roll," she shouted.

Mom pulled the curtain back slow like the peeling of a scab. There it was—a parked cop car with another pulling up right behind it. Still wearing the fur coat, she grabbed the laundry basket full of jewelry and slipped out into the dark.

A cop saw her flowing silhouette under the parking lot lights and followed her shadow into the night. Mom shot a glare over her shoulder so fast she almost gave herself whiplash. The low-hanging moon struggled through the smog, but she could see the determination on the cop's sweating face in the failed light. He was gaining on her. She could almost feel his breath on the ends of her smoke-filled curls.

Mom picked up her pace and the jewelry rattled and clanked in her arms, growing heavier with every step. Ahead of her, she looked upon a wall of cinderblocks like some kind of cement fortress. In one desperate, violent swoop, Mom launched the laundry basket full of jewelry through the air and into the cop behind her. He tumbled and she scaled the bricks, disappearing over the wall into the alley, fur coat and all.

Fear pumped through her bloodstream, but adrenaline propelled her forward. The soles of her shoes burned from the sun-scorched asphalt and she could feel it seeping through to her heels, but she kept running.

The coat weighed down on her and even her eyes felt hot. They stung and strained through the sweat that dripped down through her mascara-caked eyelashes. Her shoulders drooped in the polluted dark and she began to slide the coat down her shaking arms.

When she emerged from the alley, she saw the blood-red flashing again.

Fuck, here we go again.

Mom pushed the coat back over her bones and rushed across the street against a red light. She could hear the hurried footsteps banging against the asphalt behind her. She looked back.

One. Two. Three. Four. Five? She lost count. *Where the fuck did they all come from?* A sea of uniforms rushed toward her, but she knew where she was going. Linda, a friend of Mom's, managed a two-story apartment complex and Mom knew the layout like the back of her hand.

Her blood pumped hot through her legs and her feet felt like lead in the boiling air. Sweat collected in tiny beads right below her breasts, running down over the peaks of her ribcage and into the seams of her underwear. She prayed for wind, the tiniest breeze, anything, but there was nothing but suffocating stillness that made it hard to swallow. Her mouth tasted like stale nicotine and cloudy strands of spit webbed across her teeth.

Mom scrambled through the long hallways and the sound of her footsteps echoed off the walls. She followed the light that splashed onto the pavement from the apartment windows in lined yellow boxes, illuminating the way like torches in the dark. The scent of marijuana spread through the air from behind the barred windows.

Finally, the stairwell. She cut the corner going up the stairs and scraped the back of her hand on the rough edges of the stucco. Blood dripped over her tight knuckles and caught along the edges of her rings. The staircase was enclosed like a narrow tunnel. Mom dragged her legs up the concrete steps and leaned against the wall. She slid down onto the floor and crumbled into her knees like a balled-up piece of paper, trying to make herself small.

The stampede of footsteps seared through the hallway below her. She watched through a crack in the stairs. There was a light. A flashlight. The battery-powered stream shot through the anxious air and danced along the concrete below.

Please. Don't look up.

The circle of light grew smaller as the sound of their footsteps grew louder. They were getting closer. Mom jolted back away from the steps as if they could see her eyes flashing in the crack of the dark.

Don't look up.

She watched the toes of their shiny black boots. If they looked up, they'd see her drowning inside her fur coat.

You motherfuckers. Don't. Look. Up.

Mom closed her eyes and listened to the intertwine of their heavy footsteps below and the weighted thumping of her heart in her ears. Then she fell asleep, slipping entirely out of the deranged world she'd built around her.

She woke to a deep black silence, which was almost more unnerving than waking up in handcuffs. Folded into herself, she was a dense and damp tangle of bones. The sleeve of her fur coat was soaked red with the blood from her hand. Unraveling herself in the quiet, she stumbled down the stairs in the darkness.

Following back through the boxes of light on the concrete like a trail of breadcrumbs, she climbed through the window of Linda's apartment and slid in behind the curtain.

"Jesus Christ, Tammy. Whatcha do now? The cops are swarming. I'm talkin' barricades, helicopters, the whole thing, man."

Mom laughed, dropping the coat from her dripping-hot frame onto Linda's kitchen floor. She disappeared down the tiny hallway into the bathroom and peeled her wet clothes from her still-pulsating skin. Leaning over the sink, the cold porcelain sent a fury of relief through her bones, but she needed air.

Mom cranked the window open to the alley that ran parallel behind the apartment complex. The limbs of a neglected orange tree crawled over the wall from the other side of the alley and dropped overripe citrus onto the pale dust. The rotting flesh of fruit sifted through the ripped screen and into the bathroom.

Staring into the mirror stained with water spots, she felt as if the whole world had suddenly rested on the surface of her eyelids. Seafoam green tile dappled with spores of black mold surrounded her wet curls like a crown of rotting Spanish moss, and she struggled to keep her eyes open.

Then she remembered. The ring. A shot of adrenaline rushed through her. She looked down at the ring still secured on her middle finger. It was caked in dried blood and the diamonds looked like a deep black sky.

Turning the water on she held her still-bleeding hand under the rusted faucet. The blood dissolved into a pink stream that splattered up the edges of the sink. Mom slid the ring from her finger and washed along the tiny prongs that held the shining clusters.

The water sputtered and the flow changed from steady to rushing, pulling the ring from her jittery grasp. Mom shoved her fingers down the drain and gripped for hope at the bottom of the wet darkness, but she pulled them out, bare and empty.

Mom has told me this story before.

I'm staring at her from where I stand in the garage. I don't bother sitting down, partly because conversations with her usually don't last longer than a cigarette, but also because every surface is covered in junk that she or her desert strays probably stole. Yesterday's eyeshadow has made its way across her high cheekbones and it glitters against the dim light. Sleepless so long, she's the kind of pretty that leaves you with a blank stare. Disarming—in handcuffs, a prison jumpsuit, or here, struggling in the darkness.

A wilting Marlboro dangles between her fingers and her nails are chewed down to brittle sliver moons. The smoke blues and whirls in the dusty dark and she waves it away from my face. I notice her long narrow fingers stacked with rings, the smaller ones on top of the ones that don't fit her, so they don't fall off. Lowering my eyes to the pages spread across my lap, I scribble-scribble-scribble my thoughts before they disappear.

"Wait." Mom tucks her chaos of curls behind one ear. "Are you putting that in your book? It's embarrassing."

"Why?"

"Why? What do you mean, why? Because I'm a criminal." A self-conscious smile spreads across her face.

"It's not embarrassing. It's what happened."

"It's just, I was bad, okay? Just make sure you put that I am sorry for everything I put you through. And that I love you more than anything." She's tapping her heel against the edge of the couch. I watch the fringe of her knee-high moccasin boots sway at her feet. A nervous fidget, an impatient tapping, a perpetual sway—the long, restless hours that forever plague her.

"What are you going to call your book, anyway?"

I shrug. "I have no idea. I haven't come up with a title yet."

"How about *Don't Let This Happen To You*, or maybe *The Mom From Hell*, or what about *This Is Your Brain On Drugs*?"

I laugh a sort of closed-mouth laugh. "I'll think of something, Mom. Anyway, don't be embarrassed. It's going to be a good story, you'll see."

"Well, not for me, it ain't. All the bad things I've done. People are gonna wonder what kind of person I am."

I lower my eyes to the tin foil stains on the rug that spills out from under the couch. Feeling around in the blue with desperate hands for something to say, the quiet is like a rushing sound. The pastel desert tries to leak in from behind the blanket-covered windows, but the light fails to illuminate the expression on her face.

Finally, I speak, and my voice sounds far away.

"We all have struggles, Mom."

She leans forward in the blue dark and flicks the embers from her cigarette into an overflowing ashtray. Her long earrings make a jingling sound and I watch her eyes fill with water.

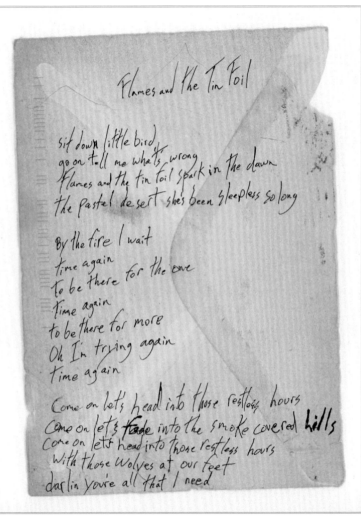

Lyrics. Perry Rhodes, 2018

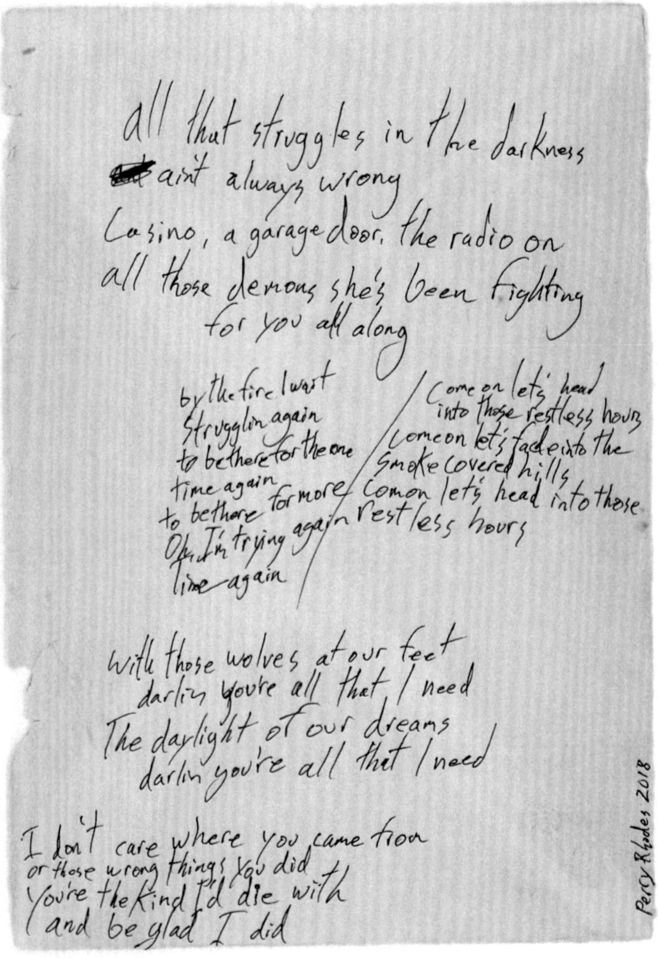

all that struggles in the darkness
~~it~~ aint always wrong
Casino, a garage door, the radio on
all those demons she's been fighting
for you all along

by the fire I wait
strugglin again
to be there for the one
time again
to be there for more
Often I'm trying again
time again

Come on let's head
into those restless hours
Come on let's face into the
smoke covered hills
Comon let's head into those
restless hours

with those wolves at our feet
darlin you're all that I need
The daylight of our dreams
darlin you're all that I need

I don't care where you came from
or those wrong things you did
You're the kind I'd die with
and be glad I did

Perry Rhodes 2018

Lyrics. Perry Rhodes, 2018

Date Street, San Bernardino, 1986

Smoke Tree Road, Victorville

Argyle Avenue, San Bernardino, 1985

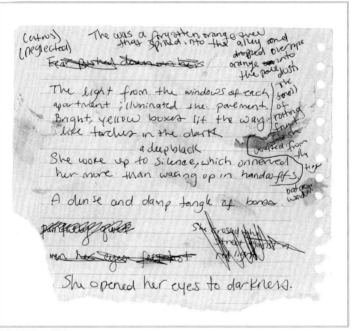

Notebook. Jessy Easton, 2019

fin

Acknowledgements

Perry, my rock, I couldn't and wouldn't have done this without you. Thank you for seeing something in me that I would've never been able to uncover on my own. Thank you for letting me drag you back to the dust of where I came from, time and time again, to take care of the ones I love and to get the courage and inspiration to tell these stories in the way they deserve to be told. Without you, these stories would've never made it to the page. Without you, this book wouldn't exist.

Mom, my beating heart, thank you for being you. You are the bright and brilliant fury of my being. Thank you for showing me that no matter how bad things get, love always has its way of shining through the darkness. Thank you for your vulnerability and raw honesty, for your strength, and for your unshakeable belief in me. I love you, infinity times the universe double root squared.

Dad, my gentle giant, thank you for loving me with all the broken pieces of your heart. Thank you for always taking care of me even when you were struggling against the worst that life had to offer. You're the strongest person I've ever known and thanks to you, I understand what it means to never give up. You're my greatest inspiration. Thank you for showing me what triumph looks like.

Thank you, dear reader, thank you for being here. Thank you for taking the time to read my words and step into the world I've lived. I appreciate you trusting me to lead you into past realms, through dark places, and into the light. I hope you found something here. Something true.